KNIGHTS & CASTLES

Judy Hindley

Illustrated by Toni Goffe

Edited by Abigail Wheatley

Designed by Sarah Cronin and John Jamieson

CONTENTS

GOING BACK IN TIME

Time travel is easy when you have a magic helmet. All you have to do is put it on, press the right buttons, and off you go. Throughout Europe you can still see the castles where wealthy barons and their knights lived.

But these real castles are often empty and half-ruined. With your time travel helmet, you can see how a castle looked with a fire roaring in the hearth and people laughing and feasting in the candlelight.

Today you are going to travel back more than 750 years, to a castle owned by Baron Godfrey, a European nobleman. When you want to come home, just press the Emergency Getaway Button on your helmet.

1. THE TIME HELMET

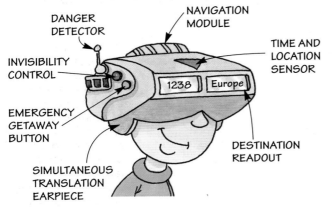

DANGER DETECTOR

NAVIGATION MODULE

INVISIBILITY CONTROL

TIME AND LOCATION SENSOR

1238 Europe

EMERGENCY GETAWAY BUTTON

DESTINATION READOUT

SIMULTANEOUS TRANSLATION EARPIECE

2. PICK A DESTINATION

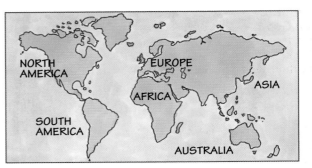

NORTH AMERICA

EUROPE

AFRICA

ASIA

SOUTH AMERICA

AUSTRALIA

As you can see, the time helmet has lots of useful gadgets. Set the Destination Readout to "Europe, 1238", and enable the Navigation Module. You're off! As you travel back in time, things begin to change...

3. GO!

1940

This is northwest Europe in 1940. There is no television because they are still quite rare. You can see that both the plane and the radio look different from ones today.

1900

Now you have gone back another 40 years things are rather different. Not everyone has electricity, so there are gas lamps and a fire. All the women wear skirts.

1800

Now you have jumped back another century. There are no gas lamps, so light comes from candles on the walls. Pianos don't exist - the instrument is a spinet.

1600

You really have come a long way now. Candles are expensive. Even glass is a luxury - notice the tiny window panes. Next stop, the Middle Ages!

THE PEOPLE YOU WILL MEET

Everyone you will meet has special duties, whether they are peasants or barons. People are born with these duties, and have little chance to change their way of life.

This is mainly because life for these people is hard and dangerous - like life on a ship or in an army. The comfort and safety of each person depends on the work of all the others.

For example, there must be strong leaders, like Baron Godfrey, to protect people from enemies and criminals. But the Baron needs people too, to work and fight for him.

Baron Godfrey is a knight and a nobleman. He is the lord of many less powerful knights. He owns a lot of land, a castle and several houses. Lady Alice is married to Baron Godfrey. She is also from a noble family. She looks after the castle and makes sure things run smoothly when the Baron is away.

BARON GODFREY **LADY ALICE**

Everyone must obey God and his king. God is obeyed through his Church, which has its own leaders. The Church's ruler is the Pope.

BISHOP

PRIEST

A priest is a religious man, who looks after the people who come to pray in his church. A bishop is in charge of lots of priests. He has a large church called a cathedral, and many lands and castles.

Baron Godfrey has many servants who must obey him and work for him. Servants do the household chores and live in the houses or castles of the people they work for.

SIMON THE KNIGHT

Simon is Godfrey's son. He will soon be a knight. Knights fight on horseback. They are usually the sons of important people, and serve a lord.

ROBERT THE SQUIRE

Robert is Godfrey's nephew. He is a squire, which is a trainee knight. It is his job to help his cousin Simon and look after his horse and weapons.

MAN-AT-ARMS

Ordinary fighting men fight on foot. A man-at-arms has a coat of arms and equipment like a knight, but no horse.

FOOT SOLDIER

Foot soldiers may have bows and arrows or other simple weapons. Both men-at-arms and foot soldiers fight for the lord who owns the land where they live.

PETER THE STEWARD

Peter, Baron Godfrey's steward, is the head of all the servants. He can read and write, and do large sums.

SERVANT

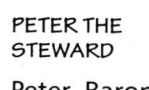

Servants are given food, clothes and a place to sleep, but they have to work hard to earn it. They even have to ask their master if they want to get married.

Peasants belong to the land owned by lords. They have to work for the lord on his land or as craftsmen. But they may get some land to farm for themselves.

PEASANT

SERF

Serfs are like slaves who work on the land. Many of them are prisoners of war. Life is hard for them.

A friar is a priest without a church or a monastery. Friars travel around the country, teaching people about God. They have to rely on people's charity to give them food, clothes and somewhere to sleep for the night.

FRIAR

MONK

NUN

Monks and nuns are people who have promised to serve God by work and prayer. They live in monasteries, which are large groups of buildings with their own churches and farms. They often live away from other people to concentrate on God.

JOURNEY TO A CASTLE

You are in Europe in the year 1238. You find yourself in rough, dangerous country. You spot a castle in the distance. All the land you can see belongs to a nobleman, Baron Godfrey.

The people who live here have to work for the Baron and obey his laws. In return he protects them. He owns several homes in different parts of his lands. Today he is coming to stay at this castle with his family, knights and servants.

The people who live nearby must bring food and supplies to the castle while the Baron is visiting. When the supplies run out, it will be time for the Baron and his followers to move on to another one of his homes.

The peasants in the VILLAGE can only leave the Baron's land if they grow rich enough to buy their freedom - or brave enough to run away to a big town.

BAAA

The stream turns the mill WHEEL and the axle of the wheel turns a heavy STONE inside. This grinds wheat into flour for making bread.

WATER MILL

Not many machines exist, apart from mills. Animals and people still do most of the hard work, like this FARMER and his OXEN working in the fields.

MEN-AT-ARMS guard the Baron and his valuables from robbers.

LADY ALICE feels sick. It's a very bumpy ride.

BARON GODFREY

THE BARON'S BEST CANDLESTICKS

Baron Godfrey takes everything valuable with him when he moves around the country, in case one of his homes is conquered while he is away. He takes food for the journey too.

Whoa there!

YAP YAP

With such a heavy load and bad roads, the carts travel very slowly - only about 30km (19 miles) a day.

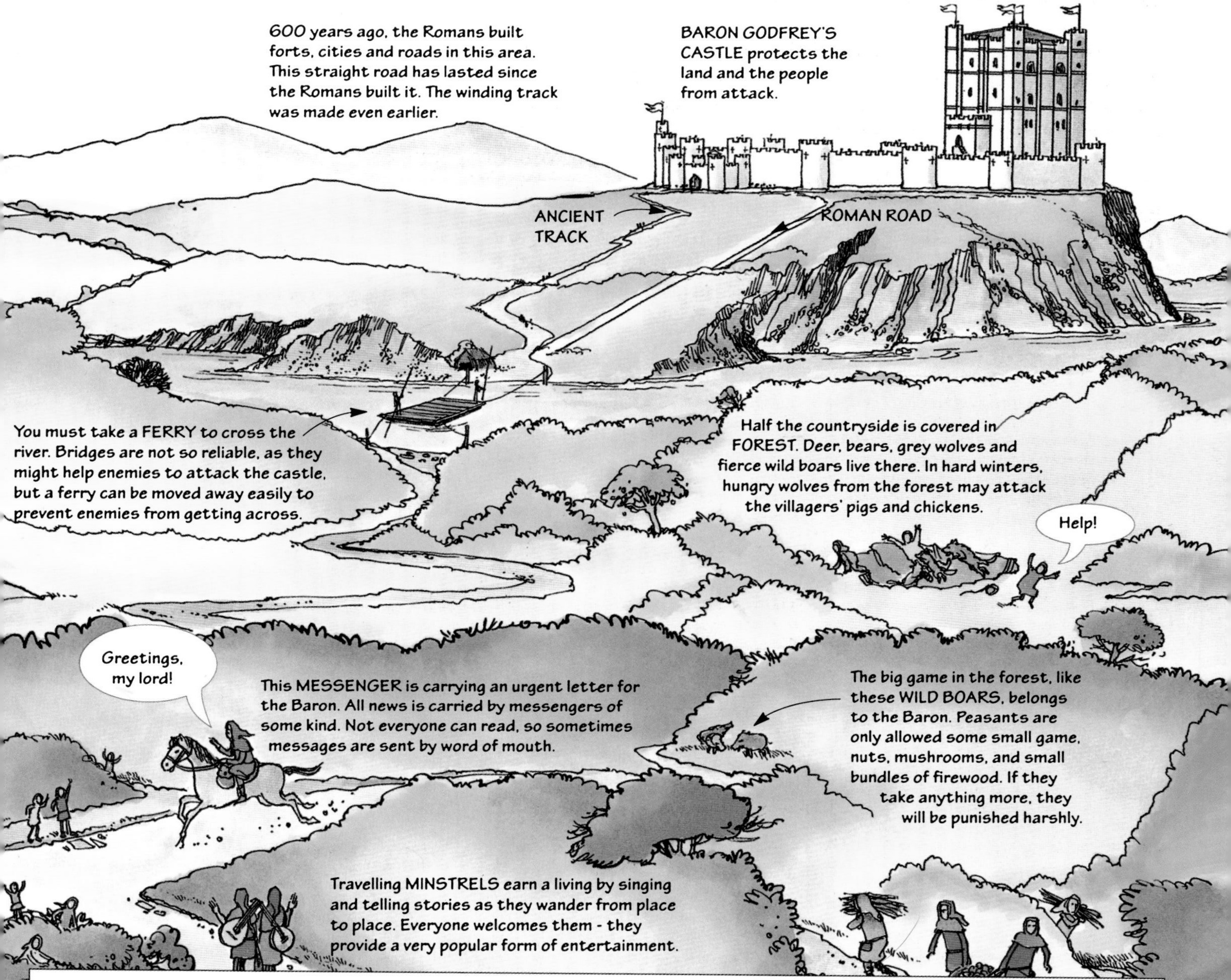

600 years ago, the Romans built forts, cities and roads in this area. This straight road has lasted since the Romans built it. The winding track was made even earlier.

BARON GODFREY'S CASTLE protects the land and the people from attack.

ANCIENT TRACK

ROMAN ROAD

You must take a FERRY to cross the river. Bridges are not so reliable, as they might help enemies to attack the castle, but a ferry can be moved away easily to prevent enemies from getting across.

Half the countryside is covered in FOREST. Deer, bears, grey wolves and fierce wild boars live there. In hard winters, hungry wolves from the forest may attack the villagers' pigs and chickens.

Help!

Greetings, my lord!

This MESSENGER is carrying an urgent letter for the Baron. All news is carried by messengers of some kind. Not everyone can read, so sometimes messages are sent by word of mouth.

The big game in the forest, like these WILD BOARS, belongs to the Baron. Peasants are only allowed some small game, nuts, mushrooms, and small bundles of firewood. If they take anything more, they will be punished harshly.

Travelling MINSTRELS earn a living by singing and telling stories as they wander from place to place. Everyone welcomes them - they provide a very popular form of entertainment.

BY LAND AND SEA

Many of the people you will meet on the road are pilgrims. They travel around visiting holy places like cathedrals and saints' tombs.

Travelling by road is not safe. Many merchants have their goods stolen by robbers and bandits, who lie in wait for them.

Sea travel is dangerous too, as no one has very good maps. Sailors steer by the stars and try to keep close to land when they can.

INSIDE THE CASTLE WALLS

Baron Godfrey's castle is very strong. It's almost impossible for an enemy to get inside. All over Europe, powerful men like the Baron are fighting each other for land. Each tries to gather many knights and build the strongest castle. This castle is well protected behind by a steep cliff, and in front by two sets of strong stone walls. The strongest part of the castle is the largest tower, known as the keep.

The entrance to the castle is like an obstacle course. To get to the keep you have to pass through four sets of gates, which are all heavily guarded. What you would find inside the castle walls is almost like a little town. There are carpenters and stonemasons to repair the walls, stables, kitchens, a well, and places to keep other animals and food.

So, if the castle was attacked, you would be able to live fairly comfortably for a few weeks inside its strong walls.

DOVE COTE

DOOR TO TOWER AND STAIRS

Paths known as WALL WALKS run along the top of the walls. Archers patrol the walls, ready to shoot enemies trying to cross the ditch, They can fire through the slits in the wall.

BOARS kept for amusement

HAY STACKS

KENNELS

Falcons are kept here

FALCON

WOOF

MAIN KITCHEN

MAIN GATEHOUSE

DRAWBRIDGE

PORTCULLIS

The BARBICAN is an extra gatehouse outside the castle's ditch. Everyone has to enter it to get inside the castle walls.

If enemies try to get in this way, the guards can trap them in the barbican and fire at them from above.

BEGGARS waiting for food or money at the gates

OUTER DOORS

BARBICAN

The Baron arrives

Move along there!

CLATTER

SENTRIES patrolling the wall walks and towers can see for miles around. They keep watch for enemies - but it can be cold work, especially in the winter.

The KEEP is the strongest part of the castle. Its walls are 3m (10ft) thick in some places, and it has no doors or windows near the ground which could help and attacker get in.

BATTLEMENTS

ABLES

BAKEHOUSE

BREAD OVEN

Lady Alice's GARDEN

BUTTRESSES help to strengthen the walls and deflect weapons.

The wooden STAIRS can be removed in case of attack.

You can see that no two ENTRANCES are straight in front of each other. An attacker could not march straight in. He would have to turn and expose his unprotected sides to attack.

PLAYING A KIND OF FOOTBALL

I wonder what's for dinner...

INNER GATEHOUSE

WELL

WOOD PILE

FISH POND

SHEEP

BAA

FRUIT TREES

ENTERING THROUGH THE CASTLE GATES

BARBICAN   DRAWBRIDGE IS LOWERED

Who goes there?

LIFTING MACHINERY

BOLT

DITCH

PORTCULLIS

First you have to get through the barbican. The guards make sure you are a friend, and then give the order to lower the drawbridge.

Next, the drawbridge swings down on big chains to make a bridge over the ditch. Guards bolt it into place and then raise the portcullis.

This is a strong iron grill to protect the doors. The guards wind it up into the room above. Finally, they unbolt the doors, and you are in!

THE KEEP

The keep is the grandest building in the castle. It was built by one of Baron Godfrey's relatives many years ago. The rooms can be smelly, cold and gloomy. When the Baron comes to stay with his family and friends, bright tapestries decorate the walls, and fires burn merrily during grand feasts. But there isn't a proper sewage system, and sometimes the terrible stink forces the Baron and his guests to leave in a hurry!

The courtyards of the castle are always busy. Traders flock from all around to sell their goods and local people come to find work and settle their arguments. Pilgrims pass through on their way to far-off churches, and barefoot preaching friars arrive, looking for a meal and shelter for the night, as they wander around Europe. All these people need a lot of looking after. The castle has its own chapel and priest, minstrels for entertainment, and lots of servants to do the work.

Lots of Lady Alice's friends live in the castle. They help her look after things, and make clothes, cushions and tapestries.

MINSTREL

Sir Gawain rode forth into battle, his shield shining brightly...

SQUIRES playing at sword-fighting

THATCHER repairing the roof

The BAKEHOUSE is an extra kitchen, where servants make bread for the big castle oven, brew beer and preserve foods for the winter.

BARON GODFREY

GUARD ROOM

SIGH

STAIRCASE

A rich SALT MERCHANT arrives to do business with the Steward. Salt is important for preserving meat, and is very expensive.

He stole my pig!

Peter is the STEWARD - an important servant. One of his jobs is settling arguments and punishing criminals.

It's my pig!

PILGRIM, telling tall tales of his travels.

Lots of little rooms, passages, stairs and cupboards are cut into the thick OUTER WALLS of the keep.

GUARDS on duty

FLUTTER

BARON'S ROOM

In her GARDEN, Lady Alice grows flowers, fruit and herbs, such as thyme, fennel, parsley, sage and hyssop, for cooking and medicine. Like many noblewomen, Lady Alice is well educated, and knows that parsley planted on Good Friday will cure sick fish.

Lady Alice spends her time reading and studying with the castle's priest, and sewing and weaving. She has maids to look after her clothes and her children. But she is also in charge of the daily running of the castle, and she looks after all the servants.

MAIDS making the bed

Lady Alice's baby

GARDEROBE (toilet)

The toilet has no plumbing - it's just a hole going down through the wall.

CHAPEL

FRUIT TREES

GREAT HALL

Emergency supplies of food and drink are kept in the STOREROOMS in the basement, in case the castle is attacked.

ARF

This man is keeping a careful record of everything going in and out of the storerooms. He is paid well because he can read and write.

CAULDRON

SNIFF

Bet you can't get it past me!

MAIDS looking after Baron Godfrey and Lady Alice's children

KICK

These women are doing the LAUNDRY. They boil it up in a big cauldron and hang it out to dry on sweet-smelling bushes in the sun.

BARON GODFREY GETS DRESSED

Before the Baron gets up, he puts on his shirt.

Next he washes his face, and then dries it.

He puts on his long tights, which are called hose.

His leather shoes fasten up with a button.

Godfrey's robe is lined with fur to keep him warm.

A useful bag for coins slides on to his belt.

LADY ALICE GETS DRESSED

Lady Alice puts on her long wool tunic...

...and a robe known as a surcoat.

A maid carefully braids Alice's long hair...

...coils the braids around Alice's ears...

...ties a piece of cloth over the braids...

...and puts a hat on top to finish it off!

WHAT OTHER PEOPLE WEAR

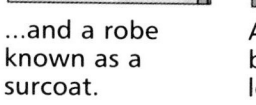 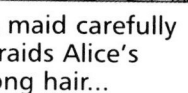 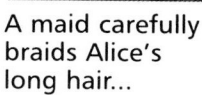  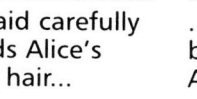

Monks and nuns spend their lives serving God and helping people. They wear long, plain clothes which are their uniform.

Young girls wear womens' clothes but leave their hair down.

Boys carry daggers in their belts from an early age.

Servants and workers wear sensible, tough clothes.

On wet days, workers wear clogs to keep their feet dry.

TAKING A BATH

This morning, Robert the squire is taking a bath. Servants fill the big wooden tub with water heated on the fire. This takes a long time, so several people have a bath at the same time. The soap is homemade from animal fat, ash and soda. It doesn't smell very nice, so flowers and herbs are sprinkled into the water.

   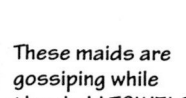

Apparently master Gerald's in love again - more poems...

These maids are gossiping while they hold TOWELS for the bathers.

FLOWERS

HERBS

GERALD

Blowing the fire with BELLOWS makes it hotter.

BUCKETS OF HOT WATER

The TUB has handles so it can be carried around. It is filled and emptied with buckets and bailers.

GOING HUNTING

Baron Godfrey spends much of his life at war with enemy barons. His knights and men-at-arms must always be ready for battle. Fighting at jousts and tournaments keeps them in shape, but in good weather they spend a lot of time hunting in the woods and fields with their hounds, hawks and horses.

There are great arguments between huntsmen and falconers over whether hounds or hawks are the bravest and most noble beasts. Their stories are told around the fire in the Great Hall, after the feasting.

But the peasants and country people do not like the hunt. Their crops are often damaged when people on a hunt ride through them, and they are not allowed to touch Baron Godfrey's game.

The MASTER OF THE HUNT plays a hunting horn made from a stag's antler. It only plays one note, but he signals with it by playing short or long blasts.

These HOUNDS are just picking up the scent of a stag. They will chase it through the forest wherever it goes... no one knows where the hunt will end up.

It is a lovely spring morning and everyone is happy. Lady Alice sings a tune as she rides along. They are hoping to catch a stag.

Springtime brings the merry flowers

SNIFF SNIFF

HUNTING HOUNDS

Lady Alice holds a FALCON. It is used for hunting other birds like pigeons.

These PEASANTS are hiding behind a tree, terrified by the sound of the hunt close by. They are poaching - catching the Baron's game. If they are caught they will be punished harshly.

TRAINING A FALCON TO HUNT

People train falcons to hunt other birds. When a falcon is young, the trainer feeds it by hand. He wears a special glove so the bird can perch on his wrist.

JINGLE

When the bird is tame, the trainer attaches a bell to its foot and ties a leash to a ring on its leg. To keep the falcon calm, the trainer puts a hood over its head.

HOUNDS AND THEIR KENNELS

A keeper makes sure the hounds are looked after well. Every day the kennel is swept and sprinkled with fresh straw. A boy sleeps in the kennel at night to keep the dogs company.

By evening the hunters have chased for hours, through brambles, and over ditches. They are tired and muddy. But the horn leads them on, until finally the stag is tired.

The hounds close in, and one hunter kills the stag quickly with a knife. The master of the hunt plays his horn to celebrate the kill.

Where are we?

YUK!

The hunters will carry the stag back to the castle to be cooked for the Baron's table. Only lords and ladies eat venison.

Good girl!

The trainer lets the bird fly short distances on its leash. He whistles to bring it back, and rewards it with food. Later, the bird learns to hunt without a leash.

If the hunt is successful, the trainer finds the falcon by following the sound of its bell. He takes the prey away and rewards the falcon with a piece of raw meat.

A TRIP TO A BUILDING SITE

As you ride with Baron Godfrey over his lands, you come upon a busy scene - another church is going up. Churches and cathedrals are springing up everywhere, as builders learn new ways to hold up the soaring roofs of these enormous buildings.

Every town competes to have the most beautiful church. Kings and noblemen, like Baron Godfrey, pay for the work in the hope that God will forgive them their cruelty and injustice.

A large church can take 50 years to finish, but if there are problems with money, it can take centuries. Even a small church like this one will take years to complete, because almost everything is done by hand.

It's coming along nicely!

Baron Godfrey and Lady Alice arrive to check on the work.

Boys, known as APPRENTICES, help the craftsmen with errands and dirty work. In exchange they get a home, food and training in the craft.

This man is making MORTAR out of sand, water and lime. It sets very hard and is used to stick the stones together.

SAND

APPRENTICES

CHIP CHIP

GRUNT

BUCKETS OF MORTAR

Craftsmen called MASONS shape each stone so it will fit into place. Then carpenters fit the roof, and glass-makers make windows to keep out the rain.

CARVING WITH HAMMER AND CHISEL

SAWING A BLOCK

GUIDELINES FOR WALLS

UGH!

Over here?

Each mason uses a special MARK, such as a cross or star, to sign his work. That way he can be sure he will get paid for each stone he cuts.

The walls go on down into the ground to give support to the building. They are called FOUNDATIONS.

These masons are using wooden shapes called PATTERNS to shape the stones for an arch. Each stone needs to be wedge-shaped, so that it presses on the stone beneath it. This way the stones lock each other into place.

The wooden roof will be covered in STONE TILES or LEAD.

Over here!

PULLEY

WOODEN SLATS FOR THE ROOF

WOODEN SCAFFOLDING

Seems to be going according to plan...

This man designed the church. He is a MASTER MASON.

To lift heavy stones, a man at the top of the wall turns a WHEEL, which winds up the ROPE.

The craftsmen you can see here come from several different countries. Lots of master masons have WANDER-YEARS, when they travel around to learn new skills.

15

A TRIP TO TOWN

Baron Godfrey's steward, Peter, is riding into town. Lady Alice has given him a huge shopping list for a feast she is arranging. She needs good wax candles, a special red dye for her new dress, and some expensive spices and silks that come from foreign countries. Peter is delighted to go.

The town is an exciting place. Thirty years ago it was just a cross-roads with a huddle of houses. All the land nearby belonged to Lord John (known as John Deadtooth). But John needed money to go on a crusade, so he rented the land to some thrifty merchants and craftsmen. Look what has happened since.

The tradespeople have prospered, and many have set up organizations called guilds which help run the town. They are like clubs, with their own special signs and customs.

CRIMINALS are hanged on the hill.

The Town Council is a group of important townspeople, elected to make rules about things like trading and refuse collection. The council meets in the TOWN HALL.

The merchant's guild meets in this GUILDHALL. Old or sick merchants live here, and there is a chapel too.

TOWN SQUARE

This man has been put in the PILLORY for selling bad fish.

The streets are not paved and they get filthy with MUD, REFUSE and animal DUNG.

The RIVER is the town's main water supply.

GROAN!

BARBER'S SHOP - the barber is also the dentist.

At night, the GATEKEEPER shuts the town GATES to keep out thieves. WATCHMEN patrol the streets to check for fires and prevent crime.

Whoa!

GATES

The GOLDSMITH'S house is well protected. It is also his shop, and because it is safe, people use it for storing valuable things, like a bank.

PETER

Peasants sometimes try to escape to a town to find a good job. If they manage to stay for a year and a day, they will be free from their duties on the land.

ESCAPING PEASANT

CHURCH

HORSE TROUGH

MARKET

Each market STALL HOLDER has to pay the town council for a permit to trade.

The CHURCH is always busy. People come here to meet and pray. The priest is well educated – he can read Latin. If criminals escape to the church, they will be safe.

PICKPOCKET

Good morrow, friends.

TEACHER

Stop!

This PILGRIM is visiting a saint's tomb in the church. He wears a cross on his back to show he is on a religious journey.

People grow food and keep chickens in their GARDENS.

The people are proud of their town's fine WALLS. They make the town look strong and important. Everyone helped to pay for the walls.

GIVING A FEAST

Today is an important festival day and the Baron is holding a feast to celebrate. In the kitchen, the servants have been working since dawn to prepare all the food.

Lots of spices and herbs are used to make the meat taste better. It's hard to keep food fresh, and it goes bad quickly. Sometimes food is scarce in the winter. A few years ago there was a famine and the poor people had to eat grass.

But today the servants are preparing lots of splendid food for the feast. The Baron will give away any leftovers to the poor.

This woman is grinding up herbs and spices with a PESTLE in a MORTAR.

GEESE from the poultry-yard

This boy turns the SPIT to make sure the meat cooks evenly. He is using an old archery target to screen him from the heat.

CAULDRON

FISH from the castle pond.

MAKING STEW

Meat is often roasted on a SPIT in front of the fire.

This pan catches the tasty meat juices.

BAKING BREAD

A fire is lit inside the oven to heat it while the dough is being made. Then the fire is raked out and the dough is put into the clean, hot oven.

After the bread is baked, the oven is still warm. It will be used to make cakes, or to dry out clothes or wood for the fire. Every bit of heat is used.

IN THE CAULDRON

BOILED CHICKENS

PUDDING IN A BAG

CARROTS

BACON

This picture shows some of the things that can be cooked in a cauldron. Later, the hot water will be used for washing up. Nothing is wasted.

IN THE GREAT HALL

At noon the tables in the great hall are laid. Baron Godfrey invites all sorts of people, including traders, wandering knights and churchmen. A feast is a good way to hear all the news.

If you're really lucky, you'll sit with the Baron at the high table. It is on a raised platform at the top of the hall. Only the important people sit here.

Four courses will be served today. The dishes include: boar's head; shellfish seasoned with marigolds; spiced beef; stuffed quarter of bear; sugared mackerel; squirrel stew, and honey cakes, if you're still hungry.

The tables are made form BOARDS resting on TRESTLES so they can be cleared away easily. Later, people will be sleeping in here.

MINSTRELS sing in between the courses. Sometimes there are jugglers or jesters, or short plays called INTERLUDES, acting out famous battles and the stories of heroes.

What's the latest from court, my lord?

More wine!

King Arthur set out from Camelot one morn in fine array

Ta-ran-ta-ra!

SERVING THE MEAT COURSE

MYSTERY PLAYS

Is that baby Jesus, Dad?

BOO! HISS!

ARF!

On special days, like today, members of town guilds act out parts of the Bible. Guilds are also called mysteries so these are called 'mystery plays'.

The performers stand on wagons so they can be seen. Then they pull their waggon to different parts of the town, and do several performances.

Most people can't read, so the plays teach them about the Bible. It's also a good chance for guilds to show off their wares on stage!

ROBERT THE SQUIRE

You will notice a lot of children around the castle. One of them is the Baron's nephew, Robert. He was sent to live with his uncle when he was six years old.

Since then, he has served as a page at the castle, leaning to be polite and obedient and fetch and carry. Now he is 14 years old, Robert can become a squire. This means he is training to be a knight one day. Robert also helps Baron Godfrey's son, Simon, who will soon become a knight. Robert must take care of Simon's weapons and help him get ready for tournaments and battles.

1. USING A CROSSBOW

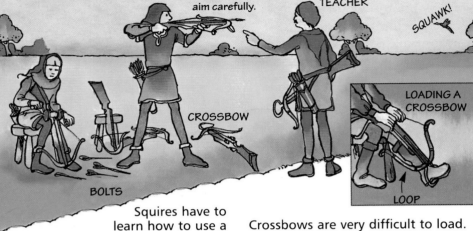

Squires have to learn how to use a crossbow. Knights never use crossbows in battle, but they do use them when they go hunting. The special arrows are called bolts.

Crossbows are very difficult to load. You have to put one foot into a loop at the base of the bow, and then pull hard with both hands to fix the bolt in place and set the bow string.

2. RIDING

Robert has to learn how to ride one-handed. This keeps his weapon arm free. He trains his horse to get used to loud noises, so it doesn't shy in a battle.

3. USING A LANCE

Here Robert is about to gallop at a rotating target, called a quintain. He has five tries to knock it down by hitting it exactly in the middle.

He holds the heavy lance against his side to keep it steady. It is important to aim the lance very carefully, otherwise it will throw him off balance.

At the last moment, he rises in his stirrups to get his whole body behind the blow. If the blow is off-target, the quintain will swing around and hit him.

4. SWORD PLAY

Now Robert and another young squire are using small, blunt swords made of wood, and little round shields called bucklers.

Robert learns to slash with the sword's edge and to ward off blows from his opponent with his sword or his buckler.

As the boys get stronger, they use heavier weapons. A real battle sword weighs 1.5kg (3.5 pounds) and it can slice through steel.

A SQUIRE'S DUTIES

A squire has to help a knight get dressed for jousts and battles.

He has to help the knight put on his chain mail shirt and other gear.

He cleans rusty chain mail by rolling it in a barrel of sand.

AT SCHOOL

A priest teaches the squires how to read and write a little. Sometimes Lady Alice reads them stories. Paper is very rare, and writing is normally done on parchment - treated animal skin. But this is expensive, so children use pointed sticks and tablets covered in wax. For calculations they have an abacus, a frame with counting balls which slide along on wires.

PRIEST

ABACUS

LADY ALICE

PRETEND JOUSTING

Take that!

WRESTLING

QUINTAIN PRACTICE

WAR GAMES

These young squires will grow up to be knights one day. Then they will have to earn their living by fighting in tournaments or even in wars. Their games are fierce and war-like. Knights must learn to be tough.

Some of them are fighting, or getting ready to learn how to joust, with wooden poles and a pretend horse and target. These squires are having plenty of fun playing outside with their rough, wooden weapons. But the sons of kings and very rich parents sometimes have beautiful model castles to play in!

SIMON BECOMES A KNIGHT

The time has come for Simon to be made a knight. His training is complete. He will be knighted along with several of his friends at a grand ceremony in the Great Hall.

First, they spend the whole night praying in the chapel. They don't eat or sleep, and they pray that God will help them to be strong and brave.

Religion is an important part of being a knight. Knights have to promise to fight for God as well as for their lord. It is their job to protect religious people, women and workers, who can't fight.

Only important fighters become knights. The rest fight without horses, on foot.

The squires pray all night in the chapel, kneeling or lying on the floor. It's freezing cold, but this helps keep them awake!

BRRR!

ROBERT

SIMON

SCRUB

SPLASH

Don't forget your sword!

SWISH

At dawn, Simon leaves the chapel and takes a bath in preparation for the ceremony.

He puts on a special white robe. This shows that he promises to be pure and faithful when he is a knight.

Carrying his sword, Simon goes to the Great Hall for the ceremony which will make him into a knight.

THE CEREMONY

Simon arrives at the Great Hall of the castle, where a crowd of knights and ladies have arrived to watch the ceremony. First, in front of everyone, Robert the squire arms Simon for battle.

1. A quilted vest and cap protect Simon from blows and from his heavy gear.

2. The chain mail shirt is heavy, but it will keep out arrows and swords.

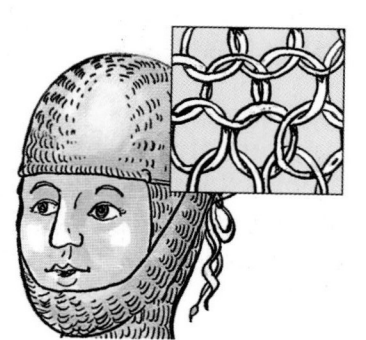

There is also a chain mail hood. Chain mail is made from linked metal rings.

4. Robert fastens the leather straps of Simon's chest protector. It is made of strong metal plates.

5. Metal shin guards go on over mail leggings to provide extra protection for the knight's legs.

6. He has arm guards and shoulder guards to shield him from an enemy's slashing sword.

7. A linen tunic goes over the top. On Simon's belt is the scabbard, where he will keep his sword.

8. The helmet hides his head completely, but it has holes for seeing and breathing.

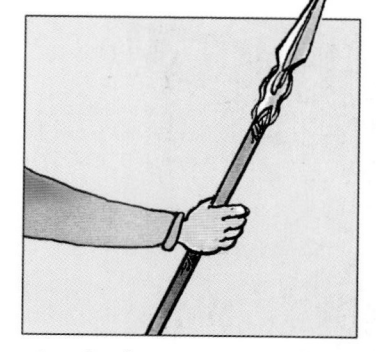

9. On his tunic and shield he wears a symbol called a coat of arms, to show other people who he is.

"The two edges of the sword show that the knight serves God and the people."

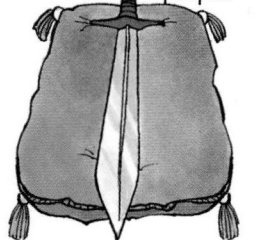

10. Now a priest blesses Simon's weapons. He explains their special meanings to the new knight.

11. The long lance shows that the knight will drive back his enemies.

Awake from evil dreams and keep watch, with faith in Christ and with virtue in your deeds.

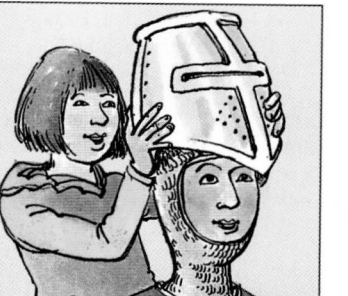

12. Now the Baron strikes Simon on both shoulders with the flat part of the sword and gives him the kiss of peace.

13. Simon has been dubbed a knight. He is given his sword and spurs which show he is now a knight.

Arise, Sir Gerald!

Now that he is a knight, Simon can dub new knights himself. He starts right away with his friend Gerald.

GOING TO A TOURNAMENT

Baron Godfrey has arranged a tournament to celebrate Simon's knighthood. At tournaments knights take part in competitions called jousts, trying to knock each other off their horses with long wooden poles called lances. Sometimes groups of knights also fight in mock battles at tournaments. These are called melees. They can get quite fierce.

Suddenly, the trumpeters play a fanfare to announce the arrival of the strange Black Knight. He is a knight errant, which means he does not have his own lands. He earns his living by fighting at tournaments. If he wins a joust, he gets his opponent's horse and weapons. If he wins the whole tournament, there is a big prize.

Today, Simon has challenged the Black Knight to a joust. He hopes he can prove his skill and show he deserves to be a knight. Simon's squire, Robert, is at his side. He is in charge of Simon's horse and other gear. A big crowd has gathered, eager to watch the jousting.

TRUMPETERS

Ta-ran-ta-ra!

THE BLACK KNIGHT

A HERALD announces the contestants and recounts their great deeds. He must be able to recognize everyone from their coats of arms.

Today we have Sir Simon, son of Sir Godfrey...

SIMON

Ladies and nobles watch the joust from special STANDS.

Simon was given this GLOVE by his cousin Anna. He is proud of it and shows it off in the joust. She is the sweetest lady he knows.

The SQUIRES watch to see if they are needed. If Simon falls off his horse or is hurt, no one but Roger is allowed to help him.

The strip of ground where the knights joust is called the LISTS.

The latest SADDLES have high backs which make it extra difficult for knights to knock each other off their horses.

SIMON FIGHTS THE BLACK KNIGHT

THRUM

The trumpet sounds to signal the start of the contest. The knights will ride past each other three times. If Simon manages to strike the top of the Black Knight's helmet or knock him off his horse, he will win a point.

CRASH!

On the first pass, Simon's lance is shattered, but he stays on his horse. He has not lost a point yet.

Squires are rubbing down the HORSES and giving them a drink of water.

Crowds of people come from miles around to watch the jousting and join in the celebrations. There are other ENTERTAINMENTS on offer for them - boxing, food stalls and feasting.

BOXERS

Pies! Hot Pies!

SPARE LANCES

PICK-POCKET

FOOD AND DRINK ARE ON SALE HERE.

The knights get ready for the joust in these TENTS.

Jousting can be dangerous. This knight has been knocked off his horse and injured badly. He may die. A priest is praying for him.

A WOUNDED knight is being helped back to his tent.

GROAN!

Keep well back!

Go on Simon!

This knight was DEFEATED in this morning's joust. He has lost his horse and his gear, and he has given his last penny to his faithful squire.

COATS OF ARMS

Each knight wears a special symbol on his shield and his clothing called a coat of arms. This symbol enables people to recognize the knight, particularly when his face is hidden by his helmet. Family members can use similar coats of arms to show they are related. The symbols can be patterns or pictures showing animals or things. Sometimes the pictures show what the knight's name means.

PEGASUS

UNICORN

SEA-HORSE

ARMS OF VON BAUM (BAUM MEANS TREE)

ARMS OF VON BRUNNEN (BRUNNEN MEANS WELL)

GRIFFIN WITH CROWN

SWIPE

Mercy!

God keep you.

By the last pass, neither of the knights has lost a point. They dismount and continue on foot.

At last the Black knight is defeated. He is at Simon's mercy. Simon can hold him prisoner if he wants to.

But Simon decides to release him. Simon's only request is to exchange horses as a reminder of the fight.

RETURN FROM THE CRUSADES

One day, a strange procession appears at the castle gates. There are tanned, weary men, and donkeys laden with heavy packs filled with strange trees, silk cloth and exotic gifts. With them is a creature that nobody has seen before - a camel.

The men look strange. Their clothes and saddles look foreign. Suddenly, Lady Alice recognizes her brother, Rudolf. He has been abroad for several years, fighting a crusade. They have all had many adventures on their way and brought back lots of things which are unknown in Europe.

Where did you get it?

Is it fierce?

What is it?

Look!

Dad - we missed you! Tell us all about your adventures!

The Holy Land is full of marvels - see this glass goblet? I saw a man make it by blowing through a pipe with his mouth!

If you feed these leaves to special worms they make silk. Want to see the worms?

This is Damask - it comes from Damascus.

No!

This tree grows delicious little fruits called apricots.

My dear brother!

Lady Alice!

How lovely!

Yes!

WHAT IS A CRUSADE?

A crusade is a religious war. The most famous crusades were at the time of knights and castles. They were wars in which Christian armies from Europe tried to conquer Jerusalem and the Holy Land (where Jesus had lived). They started in 1095. For centuries, European Christians had allies close to the Holy Land. The Byzantine Christians were friendly and helped European pilgrims to visit the places where Jesus had lived.

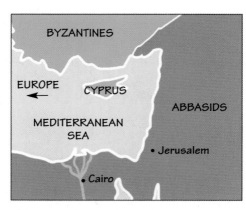

BYZANTINES

EUROPE

CYPRUS

ABBASIDS

MEDITERRANEAN SEA

• Jerusalem

• Cairo

This map shows the Holy Land around the year 1070.

The Holy Land was ruled by different groups of Muslims including the Abbasids. They all followed the teachings of the Prophet Mohammed. But they respected the Christians and made them welcome. But, in the 11th century, the Holy Land was conquered by a group of people called the Seljuk Turks. They were also followers of Mohammed. But they were not sympathetic to the Christians, and they forced the Byzantines to leave the Holy Land.

CRUSADERS' TALES

Lady Alice's brother Rudolf tells of his adventures on crusade.

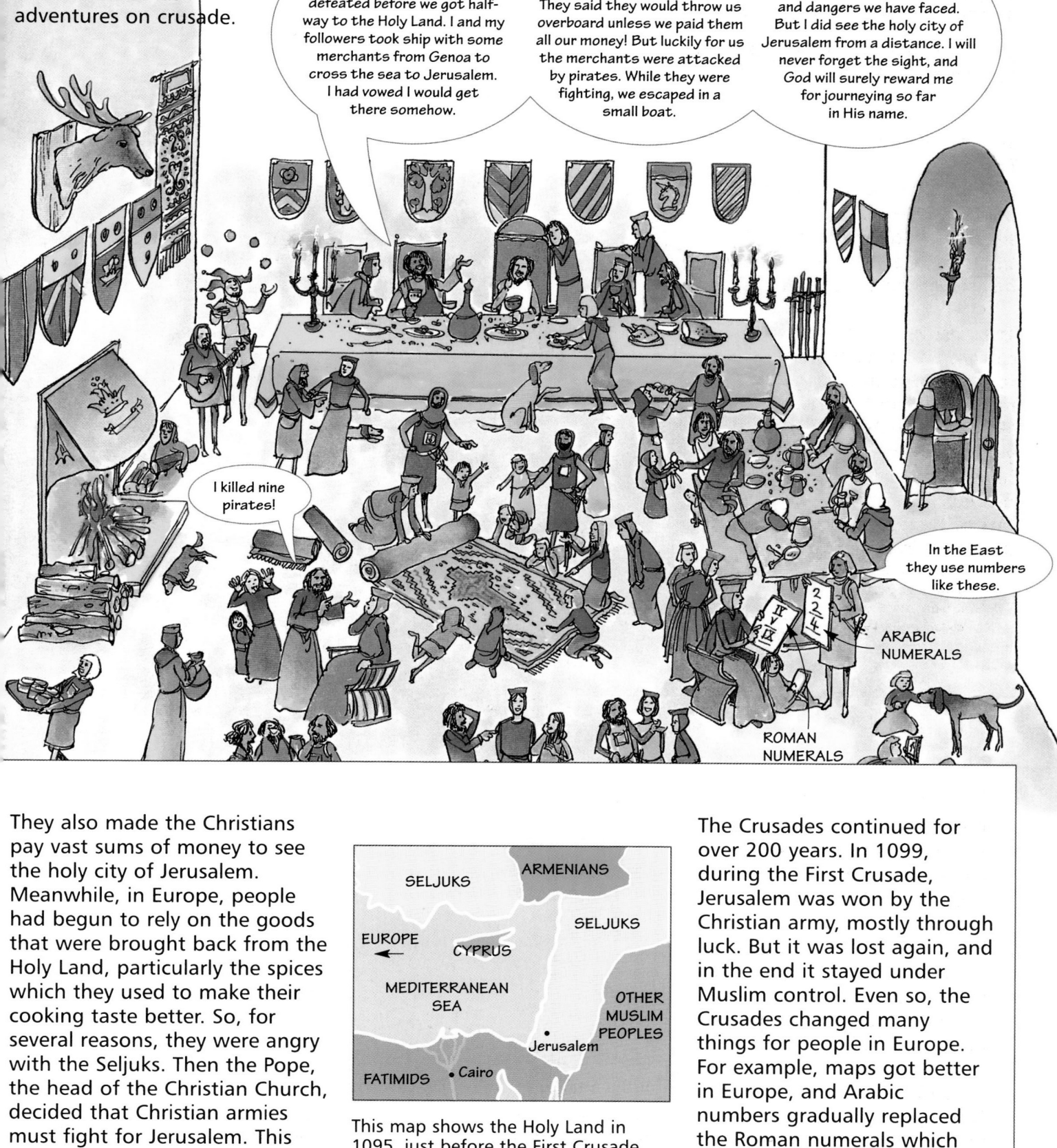

You must have heard that we were defeated before we got half-way to the Holy Land. I and my followers took ship with some merchants from Genoa to cross the sea to Jerusalem. I had vowed I would get there somehow.

But one night the merchants took us prisoner. They said they would throw us overboard unless we paid them all our money! But luckily for us the merchants were attacked by pirates. While they were fighting, we escaped in a small boat.

Ah, you wouldn't believe the difficulties and dangers we have faced. But I did see the holy city of Jerusalem from a distance. I will never forget the sight, and God will surely reward me for journeying so far in His name.

I killed nine pirates!

In the East they use numbers like these.

ARABIC NUMERALS

ROMAN NUMERALS

They also made the Christians pay vast sums of money to see the holy city of Jerusalem. Meanwhile, in Europe, people had begun to rely on the goods that were brought back from the Holy Land, particularly the spices which they used to make their cooking taste better. So, for several reasons, they were angry with the Seljuks. Then the Pope, the head of the Christian Church, decided that Christian armies must fight for Jerusalem. This was the First Crusade.

This map shows the Holy Land in 1095, just before the First Crusade.

The Crusades continued for over 200 years. In 1099, during the First Crusade, Jerusalem was won by the Christian army, mostly through luck. But it was lost again, and in the end it stayed under Muslim control. Even so, the Crusades changed many things for people in Europe. For example, maps got better in Europe, and Arabic numbers gradually replaced the Roman numerals which had been used there before.

THE CASTLE IS ATTACKED

Baron Godfrey has been arguing over a piece of land with another local ruler, Lord John. Now John and his army have attacked the Baron's castle.

Luckily there is plenty of food stored inside the castle. Local people have brought their families, animals and household goods into the castle for safety.

Lord John's army is already breaking down the outer walls with great siege towers and battering rams. But the keep is still strong.

The local people have taken shelter in the castle. Now they rush into the inner enclosure for safety. Homes and animals are left behind.

KEEP

I wish I could fight too, just like the Lady of the Golden Banner, leading her army on Crusade...

ANNA

INNER COURTYARD

WAAAA

To the keep!

SCOOP

Quick!

Wooden SHELTERS are being fitted quickly to the walls. In them the defenders can get out over the walls to drop things on the attackers. They can also shoot arrows safely from inside.

SIEGE WEAPONS

When an army traps its enemies in a strong place, it is called a siege. The people inside cannot easily get out or get help, but the attackers cannot easily get in. If the people inside have enough food and water, they can survive, but only for a while. They hope that another army will come to help them in time, or that the attackers will run out of supplies and have to leave. But the attacking army wants to finish the siege quickly, before this can happen. There are lots of weapons each side can use to try to win more quickly.

TRUNDLE

SIEGE TOWER

If the attackers fill up the castle ditch, they can roll a huge wooden tower, called a siege tower, up to the walls. Then they can climb up it and go over the wall.

AAGH!

SHELTER FOR TUNNELERS

The attackers can dig a tunnel under the castle walls. They prop the tunnel up with wooden supports. When they burn these supports, the wall above collapses.

LORD JOHN ATTACKS

"Retreat!"

By the second day of fighting, Lord John's men have undermined the wall of the inner courtyard. The wall crumbles and the Baron's men run for the safety of the keep.

VICTORY

"Take that!"

That night, Simon and a band of knights creep out of a secret gate at the back of the keep. Silently, they set fire to the enemy's camp. Lord John's men try to fight but many flee without their weapons. In the final battle, many man are killed. The Baron himself is wounded, but the castle is saved.

THUD!

RAM

Attackers can try to batter down the walls with a battering ram - a heavy log with a metal point.

MANTLET

Hiding behind movable wooden shelters called mantlets, attackers can carry ladders up to the castle. They can then use these to climb over the walls into the castle.

ARROW SLIT

WINCH

FOOT LOOP

CROSSBOWS

The people defending a castle can fire or throw things from the castle walls at the attackers. Archers are protected by raised sections of the wall and fire through arrow slits.

OOPH!

LONGBOW AND ARROWS

The English have learned to use a bow called a longbow. It can be loaded much more quickly than a crossbow, which has to be loaded with a winch or using a foot loop.

A CASTLE MAP

Now reset your time travel helmet to take you back to the present day. But before you go home, adjust the Flight Control and hover above Europe for a moment. You can see where the finest castles can still be found.

FINLAND

NORWAY

Akershus

Turku

SWEDEN

ESTONIA

Visborg

Riga

Kalmar

LATVIA

DENMARK

Hammershus

LITHUANIA

Glücksburg

Trakai

Marienburg

NETHERLANDS

BELARUS

Kildrummy

Edinburgh

Alnwick

Carrickfergus

BRITAIN

Muiderslot

GERMANY

POLAND

IRELAND

Trim

Conisbrough

Caernarfon

Harlech

Loevenstein

Wartburg

Wawel

UKRAINE

Nenagh

Ferns

Castle
Rising

Chepstow

Marksburg

Karlstejn

Hukvaldy

Caerphilly

Tower of
London

Gravensteen

BELGIUM

Burg
Eltz

CZECH REPUBLIC

SLOVAKIA

Restormel

Arques

Kaiserburg

AUSTRIA

Sárospatak

Château Gaillard

Coucy

Gisors

Burghausen

Salgo

ROMANIA

La Roche
Guyon

Etampes

SWITZERLAND

Hochosterwitz

Forchtenstein

HUNGARY

Angers

Chillon

Kropfenstein

Bled

Bran

Langeais

Aigle

Castel del
Buonconsiglio

SLOVENIA

Hunedoara

Loches

FRANCE

Fenis

Castelvecchio

CROATIA

BOSNIA-
HERZOGOVINA

Villandraut

Gradara

YUGOSLAVIA

BULGARIA

Aigues-mortes

ITALY

Carcassonne

Rocca
Maggiore

MACEDONIA

Roumeli
Hissar

Bragança

SPAIN

CORSICA

Castel
Sant'Angelo

Castel del
Monte

ALBANIA

Anatoli-
Hissar

Alcázar of
Segovia

SARDINIA

Castel Nuovo

GREECE

Torre de
Belém

Belmonte

Bellver

Castello di
Lombardia

Bodrum

Monteagudo

Silves

Alhambra
of Granada

Paterno

SICILY

Rhodes

PORTUGAL

CRETE

TUNISIA

MOROCCO

ALGERIA

LIBYA

EGYPT

MOLDO

HOW CASTLES GROW

A castle is a kind of fortress where people could live, protected from their enemies. The first castles in Europe were probably built around the ninth century. There were lots of things to think about when building a castle, to make it safe from attack.

People often tried to build castles in places which were naturally defended by water or by high ground. If a site was chosen well, there were lots of different ways of protecting the castle. But these protections could also be built in, by digging a moat, or by building a high mound.

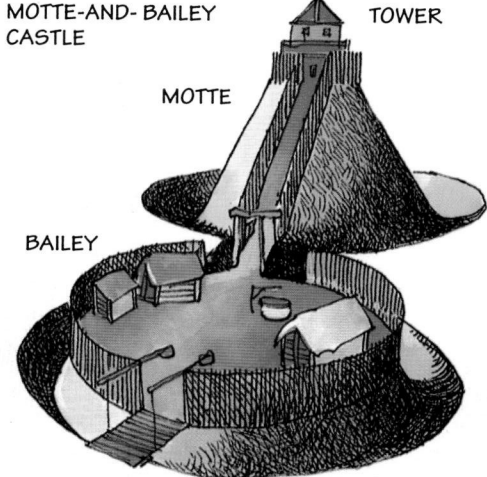

MOTTE-AND- BAILEY CASTLE

TOWER

MOTTE

BAILEY

Motte-and-bailey castles were often used in the 11th century. The safest place was in the small wooden tower, on top of the high, steep mound known as the motte. In times of less danger, people could live in the bailey, the larger, lower enclosure.

KRAK DES CHEVALIERS, IN SYRIA

Wood was easy to use when a castle needed to be built quickly. But when castle builders had the time and money, they could use stone instead. Some wooden castles were replaced by stone ones later on, to make them stronger and more impressive.

Castle builders learned a lot from the castles they saw on the Crusades - like Krak des Chevaliers, which has several rings of walls to make it harder to attack. It also has towers along its walls, so the defenders can see and shoot at their enemies more easily.

CAERPHILLY, IN WALES

Many later European castles adopted these features to add extra protection. For example, Caerphilly Castle has two rings of walls. Castles like this were very strong and hard to capture.

Protection gradually became less important over the centuries, and many castles were left to crumble away. But people still enjoy looking at castles, and some people live in them even today. Castles are often very beautiful buildings, and they remind people of how life used to be long ago.

COUCY, IN FRANCE

RUSSIA

TURKEY

Edessa

Kyrenia

Saône

CYPRUS

Krak des Chevaliers

Kolossi

SYRIA

Sidon

LEBANON

Chastel Pèlerin

ISRAEL

Kerak

Montréal

JORDAN

INDEX

Usborne Publishing would like to thank the following for their help with this book:
Peter Vansittart, Angela Littler, Nicholas Hall, Gillian Evans, Michele Busby and Philippa Wingate.
Additional illustrations on page 2 are by Stephen Cartwright, and on pages 5 and 19 are by Joseph McEwan.

First published in 1976 and revised 1997 and 2003 by Usborne Publishing Ltd,
83-85 Saffron Hill, London EC1N 8RT, England.
www.usborne.com